Questionable Autism

By:

Susan Louise Peterson

Award Winning Autism Author

All rights reserved © 2014 by Susan Louise Peterson

No part of this book may be reproduced or transmitted in any form or by any means, graphic, electronic, or mechanical, including photocopying, recording, taping, or by any information storage retrieval system, without the written permission of the author.

Questionable Autism

Susan Louise Peterson

Contents

PREFACE	vii
Prologue	ix
ACKNOWLEDGEMENTS	xi
INTRODUCTION	xiii
Chapter 1: Questionable Autism Screening & Testing	1
Chapter 2: Questionable Autism Professional Issues	13
Chapter 3: Questionable Autism Parenting Issues	25
Chapter 4: Questionable Autism Practices	37
Chapter 5: Questionable Autism Research Links	49
Chapter 6: Questionable Autism Field Issues	61
RECOMMENDED READING for AUTISM	75
INDEX	77
Afterword	83

PREFACE

When I wrote my first book on autism I started to ask myself why I did this. After all, autism is one of the most controversial fields of study where there is a vast array of opinions about the subject. There are mountains of information on autism so it is confusing to both parents and professionals. I wrote my second book on the topic of autism, *Questionable Autism* because I felt there were so many questions that should be asked. These questions open the door for us to explore new issues and readdress some of the pressing problems and concerns that seem to plague the field of autism and special needs identification. This book is written to focus on some questionable aspects of autism related to practice, research, diagnostic and parenting issues.

When questioning autism, there starts to be a sense that some of these considerations are quite simple. Sometimes, a practice in real world schools may need to be readjusted or thought through in a different way. Maybe a different approach could be used with a child who has autism characteristics that better meets his or her needs. Yet, at other times a policy change in a school district could be questioned as to how it benefits children with autism. Teachers and professionals working with children in an autism classroom could be tapped for strategies that would help ease school adaptability. Most importantly, parents who spend time with their children on a daily basis can contribute practical and useful ideas that may enhance the child's educational experience. *Questionable Autism* brings up some of these practices and possibilities that could be questioned as possible future changes and adjustments in the field of autism.

Prologue

Having seen thousands of autism cases pass through my life as a school psychologist, I, at times have professionally questioned some of these cases.

When I hear of teachers out in the field say things like 'that child should have never been diagnosed with autism or placed under an autism eligibility category' I start to think back on a few of the questionable cases. There are special education professionals who are specifically trained in techniques for home observation assessments. There are times I have heard these professionals say 'the first ten minutes the child seemed typical with appropriate play and eye contact, but then behaviors became more atypical or unusual' so the team may go with autism.

The need to take time and collect more information on the child is often rushed by special education deadlines to complete an assessment and develop an educational plan in a short time frame. Parents are watching the child develop and then begin to question if the child's strengths, abilities and traits were noticed in the educational evaluations and testing assessments presented. *Questionable Autism* was written to help parents and professionals as they begin to question some of these issues, challenges and practices in the field of autism.

ACKNOWLEDGEMENTS

I am grateful to the many professionals who approach autism concerns from different points of view. This has helped me see there is more than one way to look at delays and autism concerns and see the many facets of social, medical, environmental and educational issues that impact a child's life.

I would also like to thank my husband and twin daughters for their continued support and patience with my life as a writer. I cannot express how deeply important this is to me as I try to balance my life as a wife, mother, friend, school psychologist and a writer.

I appreciate the professionalism and kindness of working with Jim Grinnell at Vilnius Press who remains interested in the field of autism and does a superb job in helping authors and educators express their professional concerns.

INTRODUCTION

As a school psychologist I have listened to parent concerns related to autism on a daily basis. Sometimes, parents would question whether their children really have autism. The concern may stem from a variety of misguided efforts, inaccurate information or uncertainty about the information presented by professionals. As parents face this information on autism it is sometimes troubling to them because the focus seems to be on a certain aspect or characteristic of the child and not always a full picture of the child's struggles, weaknesses, abilities and skills. The book, *Questionable Autism* is focused on opening the door to practical concerns, real world practices and a wide variety of autism issues that could be questioned.

Information overload about autism can be confusing because it is so highly publicized and sparks controversy even from a brief comment or speculation. There are some professionals who view autism as a specific disorder with one explanation for its cause and a certain prescribed treatment to address it. For other professionals, the world of autism is not so certain and may be a component of more than one element or many factors that contribute to autism. This confusion about autism is one more reason to address some of the issues in the book *Questionable Autism*.

Chapter 1
Questionable Autism Screening & Testing

As a school psychologist I am involved with assessing children for autism and developmental delays. The first chapter deals with many issues related to screening and testing of children for autism. It includes looking at whether one test or a variety of tools should be used to determine autism eligibility and whether a one person or team approach should be considered in assessing autism. The question of the length of an assessment for autism is also explored and how a short assessment may miss key elements of the child's behavior on a specific day. In addition, questions are raised regarding outdated and updated testing protocols used for autism assessment in daily settings. The testing experience of the professionals assessing for autism is also discussed.

Autism screening is another area covered as well as screening approaches used by some agencies and school districts. There is a look at how to view screening instruments and note that they are not considered a full assessment for autism. There is an overview of the reporting of scores related to autism and how different school districts may report on information related to autism for their eligibility meetings and reports. It is important to note that school districts and agencies have varied approaches in the test methods used, the number of test instruments used in autism assessments and these different organizations can use different approaches when assessing children for autism. It is hoped this chapter will open up many issues related to screening and testing in the autism area.

Questionable One Test or Method

There is one philosophical idea of autism which emphasizes that no single educational testing instrument or single medical test should be used to diagnose or determine autism eligibility. I think this philosophy is presented because autism is looked at in terms of an abundance or cluster of behaviors or characteristics. If only one instrument is used (like a parent type of checklist) and this instrument is overrated or underrated by the parent it could provide a questionable picture of whether the child has autism. There are different testing methods used by both doctors and testing professionals in the schools. Some instruments are developed with statistical norms related to the number of behaviors or characteristics a child is presenting while other instruments may be informal observation tools or teacher made checklists. Since many children with autism characteristics have trouble communicating and socially expressing themselves there are often parent interviews as a part of the testing procedure. Some medical doctors watch the child for a limited time and have a brief interview with the parent to determine autism. Other medical professionals may conduct more extensive evaluations and testing procedures to explore how the child relates to others. School districts may have different methods of testing or evaluating for autism. For example, some school districts require professionals to use at least two instruments (one by the speech therapist and the other by a school psychologist) when an autism question arises in an evaluation to clarify whether the child is showing or not showing the traits of autism.

Questions to consider:
Was my child evaluated for autism using only one method or were multiple methods use to determine autism eligibility?

Did the testing give a full picture of the child's characteristics or was only limited information obtained on the child's abilities to communicate and interact socially?

Questionable One Person Versus Team Approach

There are parents who feel that if one doctor or school professional says their child has autism that it is definitely the best descriptor of the child. However, there are many others who could question that person's expertise and experience working with children who have autism characteristics. Especially since children with autism characteristics present with a spectrum of behaviors and the professional lacking training may miss some of the more subtle traits in the child. I think that is why I have emphasized a team approach when evaluating autism. The team approach helps in recognizing if the child presents with an abundance of characteristics or there are just a few quirky or unusual traits in the child. Multiple team members may see different behaviors, speech patterns and responses or reactions from the child. Sometimes a child is cold and withdrawn in one part of the assessment and then warms up later with other staff members. The child who refused to complete a task early in the day may be more responsive and complete a test or assessment activity after a warming up period. Therefore, the multi-team member approach gets a broader picture of the child than would be presented from only one person testing or observing the child. If the one person conducting the assessment writes a brief report with limited details and documentation of the child's autism characteristics it could open the door for many questions related to the child's initial autism eligibility in a school program and treatment issues from a medical perspective.

Questions to consider:
Did my child obtain an autism evaluation by one professional or multiple team professionals?

What characteristics of autism were noted by the professional and were these limited remarks or based on a substantial observation and evaluation of my child?

Questionable Length of Autism Assessment

Sometimes a parent is confused because a diagnosis of autism or autism eligibility is from a person who has conducted the autism assessment for a short length of time. The professional may have short timed the assessment because of an overload of cases or be in a hurry to attend an eligibility meeting. This is not to say that some medical and educational professionals may not have a good eye for autism characteristics. In some cases, a short assessment may still be accurate if the professional has a strong knowledge of autism and experience working with children who have autism symptoms and signs. However, there can be problems if the one person diagnosing or determining autism eligibility has limited knowledge about the subject of autism. The short autism assessment may miss key characteristics the child is presenting on a particular day. If the assessment is too rushed, a picture of how the child communicates when attempting to reach for a toy or obtain an object from another person may go unnoticed. In the same way, a short assessment may not include a look at how the child responds to different people in the assessment office. For instance, does the child look when someone comes in the assessment office or does the child even respond when his or her name is called by the examiner.

Sometimes a child may respond on the first attempt, but other children may only respond to a question or request after several attempts. If the length of assessment time is too short some characteristics or traits of autism may not be noticed.

Questions to consider:
Did the professional stay with the child long enough to see how the child responded to requests or initiated play or social interaction activities?

Did the professional spend enough time to interact with the child in free play and structured tasks as well as take time to interview parents or guardians of the child?

Questionable Outdated Test Protocols

Once in a while I will hear a parent say that an early childhood agency administered an autism type of checklist, instrument or questioneer and found the child had some autism characteristics. A few months later another agency or project determined the child did not have an abundance of autism characteristics. One reason for this may be that the agencies used different testing protocols and that may be the difference in the autism eligibility results. Sometimes the same testing instrument company will come out with a new test edition or a newer version of the same test. The child tested with the earlier version may have meet the autism eligibility. If the child is given the newer version of the test instrument he or she may not qualify for an autism eligibility as the scoring of the testing protocol may be different. This is very confusing for parents who sometimes don't understand many of the components of the testing procedures. Sometimes the parents may need an additional explanation of the differences of the testing protocols and the differing scores the child obtained from the testing. It can be devastating for parents to receive the news that a child has or does not have autism especially if there are conflicting test results.

Professionals must take time to explore why testing results were varied from different times and locations. There can also be concerns presented in how testing protocols were administered and what techniques were used to engage or observe the child. As well, parent directions regarding testing protocols are explained more clearly by some professionals than others.

Questions to consider:
Did the parent understand the directions and guidelines of a testing protocol before answering questions about autism characteristics in his or her child?

Were scoring differences in test protocols explained so the parent has an adequate understanding of why the test scores varied in relation to an autism eligibility?

Questionable Updated Protocols

Professionals in the social sciences, behavioral areas and educational fields are often overwhelmed with numerous cases, issues and responsibilities of their jobs. As a result, sometimes the protocols being used become outdated and not current or updated. The stressed out professional may not have bad intentions, but simply may not have taken time to research and find that a new protocol has been developed by the testing company. School districts are sometimes under budget constraints and do not order new test kits for an extended period of time. When test kits are ordered there may be a time lapse as to when the new testing protocols are distributed to school psychologists, testing professionals and other professionals in the field. A child may be tested for autism with an outdated protocol or scoring procedures that have been revised. This is bothersome to many parents who get an autism diagnosis from a doctor or agency and then get a different testing result from another professional. Parents, then start to question the results related to the tests that were used and the scoring of those tests. Professionals have an obligation to stay undated in their fields with testing materials and protocols. It is sometimes a difficult balance for professionals who often struggle with time management and overcrowded centers of children waiting to be tested for possible developmental delays and autism concerns. There have also been errors reported in testing norms and publication manuals that could result in incorrect scoring or a child being eligible or ineligible for an autism setting.

Questions to consider:
Is my child being tested with the most updated testing protocols to determine if autism characteristics exist?

If changes were made or updated on a testing protocol would it change my child's eligibility of autism in the school setting?

Questionable Test Experience

The professionals administering a checklist, instrument or observation may have different levels of training and experience. These factors certainly influence the quality of the autism assessment. For instance, an inexperienced professional may not catch a child's 'fleeting' eye contact or hand mannerisms that an experienced professional would spot instantly in an assessment. This experience or lack of experience could influence how an instrument or observation form is administered and scored. The child's task completion could be viewed differently by professionals. A child lining up toy cars can be looked at positively by a professional as the child is learning to sort or categorize items. Sometimes a professional will ask a child why he or she moved the car. If a child says an answer like 'to put all the blue cars together,' it may be viewed as a reasonable explanation of lining up the cars. On the other hand, lining up cars can be seen as an autism characteristic when done in a more ritualistic or routine manner that can almost appear rigid if even one car is moved or adjusted in the lined up cars. Savvy experienced professionals may catch these unusual or restricted types of behaviors that an inexperienced professional may not notice. The professional with more training may also be pointing out the specific characteristics of autism to the parent throughout the testing session and this helps the parent see what observations the professional is making. It can help parents see if the professional was learning toward an autism eligibility or if other delays stood out in the child.

Questions to consider:
Was my child assessed for autism from an experienced professional who has training working with children with autism characteristics?

Were autism signs and possible characteristics noted by the professional in the course of the assessment or when results were discussed?

Questionable Autism Screener Claim

Sometimes parents will mention at an early childhood assessment that they took a screener on the internet and that the child definitely has autism. Although a screener may be helpful in recognizing some characteristics of autism, it is not a full assessment. Many of these screeners often have a disclaimer that it is only a screener and further evaluation is needed to fully diagnose autism or another condition. I have looked at some of these screeners on the internet and I do notice that at times some of the items or characteristics are the same items that would find a child meeting the eligibility of developmental delays or a speech and language impairment. Parents must be cautious not to make too many assumptions about autism until they confer with professionals who work with children in these areas. A screener is really used to examine or look at the possibility of the presence of autism characteristics. A screener would not the viewed as the final answer or determination for a child's eligibility of autism in the school setting. Professionals in the school, medical and agency settings may need to give a stronger explanation to parents to help them understand that a screener just provides a brief snapshot of some of the characteristics of the child. I think of a screener as a quick and simple way to obtain some information about the child, but a full evaluation is much more involved and detailed so that a broader picture of the child can be seen by the parent and the professionals working with the child.

Questions to consider:
Were autism concerns based totally on a screener or were other observations of the child's communication and social interactions used in the evaluation?

Was a full evaluation completed on the child after the screener was given to determine if the child has autism or other possible delays?

Questionable Screening Approaches

Some agencies screen all children in the agency for autism whether or not the child specifically had autism concerns. Although, this might sound beneficial in some ways because it helps spot children with real autism concerns early, it may actually have some negative side effects. For example, it puts the idea in a parent's mind that the child really does have autism because it is simply mentioned to the parent. Many parents don't understand that a screener is not a full assessment for autism. There are also some clinics that then do a complete and full autism assessment if anyone on the team (including the parent or professional) even mentions the word autism. What happens is that many autism assessments are conducted on children who actually just have developmental delays. In addition, there are some children who just have speech delays or a speech and language impairment, but are immediately tested for autism. In a world where there are tons of children waiting to be tested and evaluated there becomes a backed up educational system. In some states, there are very long waiting lists and children who need to be assessed for autism will never be tested because children without autism characteristics are also being tested for autism. This is bothersome to me as a professional when we are assessing every child for everything with a complete and full assessment. In a world with budget cuts and more efficient program funding allocations to education, shouldn't there be more considerations before we test so many children for autism with a complete assessment?

Questions to consider:
Did the parent ask the professionals what specific behaviors would trigger a red flag for possible autism and warrant testing in autism?

Did the professional explain the difference between a brief screener for autism and a full autism assessment to the parent?

Questionable Reporting of Scores

There are many different autism instruments, scales, checklists and autism observation tools. Some of these instruments report actual scores and may indicate a probability or likelihood that a child has autism characteristics or not. However, some other instruments do not report a specific score to parents, but rather just provide a description of an observation experience with the child. I have noticed at eligibility meetings that some parents are questioning or would like to know more information on how an instrument is used to determine if a child has autism characteristics. Basically parents want to know how the information obtained from an interview or observation was used to specifically find the child with an autism eligibility. Parents also challenge some of the autism descriptions. For example, an autism observation may describe the child as not making eye contact and then a parent challenges this statement by saying 'he makes eye contact all of the time.' Sometimes professionals have to refocus the parent back to the actual day and time of the assessment and their observations from a specific setting and time.

What makes this complicated is that most standardized tests provide an actual score so professionals and parents can see the child's delays or deficits in some type of scale ranging from high to low scores. Parents then are confused when no score is provided and a simple description of a child's behavior and interactions is used to determine an eligibility that will impact the child's education and future plans.

Questions to consider:
What types of scores or ranges indicate a high or low probability of autism from the instrument used to assess the child for autism?

How did the professional determine if the child has autism if no test scores were reported on a particular instrument?

Questionable Report Information

School districts have different ways they report autism testing and results in educational eligibility reports. There are great variations in how much information is included in the reports for teachers and parents. If the information reported is too complex and complicated parents may have difficulty understanding what the report means. On the other hand, if the report information is too brief, there may not be enough details for the teacher to develop an educational program for the child. There are some school districts that use the same template or report for all children who have autism or an educational eligibility. Other school districts allow the school psychologist and team to creatively write their own reports. However, some school districts have very limited types of reports which are like a shell that just reports scores from the testing. It seems like it would be hard to develop present levels and objectives for the student's learning program if no observations or descriptions are provided with the test scores. Special education teachers designing the educational program for a student with autism would have difficulty knowing the specific areas the child needs help in as he or she goes to school. In particular, if the child has very specific behaviors that need to be addressed in the classroom a detailed description of the child's behavior should be noted in the report. The autism characteristics that impact the child and how he or she uses practical communication and social interaction should also be noted so the teacher can address these concerns as he or she develops goals for the child.

Questions to consider:
What do the testing scores mean and was the parent provided with a description to understand how the testing indicated autism?

Can you help me, as a parent, understand how my child has autism when only limited information was provided in the report?

Chapter 2
Questionable Autism Professional Issues

There are a broad range of professional issues that impact the field of autism. This chapter includes discussions regarding whether a parent seeks a medical diagnosis of autism or an educational eligibility of autism and the issues involved in these decisions. Other professional issues discussed include the knowledge or lack of knowledge of the professional in the autism field and how the professionals can be focused in only one area. Sometimes professionals have such specialized training that it limits their vast knowledge of other conditions or syndromes that may share similar characteristics of autism. In addition, autism descriptions and eligibility issues are discussed in the chapter.

An interesting professional issue discussed in this chapter is related to autism consultation. This type of consultation could really benefit families if education and medical professionals would collaborate more on the varying aspects of child's case or profile. Parents are hearing many different ideas from professionals so consultation and collaboration between the professionals may help answer questions and resolve simple issues related to the health and education of the child. There are also issues related to inconsistent information given to parents that leave them in confusion or in a state of uncertainty about understanding autism. This chapter examines the varying focus of different professional observations. Finally, the chapter considers the rise of autism cases as well as autism as a lifelong disability.

Questionable Diagnosis or Eligibility

I wish it were a perfect world in determining a diagnosis or eligibility of autism, but unfortunately it is not so simple. Sometimes a child has a medical diagnosis of autism, but the school district professionals just don't see it and go for an ineligible checkmark for the eligibility of autism. At other times, the doctor may not see autism and the school district professionals see tons of autism characteristics and go with an autism eligibility. I have seen a few doctors who collaborate with school district professionals and ask to see the school district eligibility report before making a firm diagnosis of autism. The bottom line is that professionals have varying opinions about autism. I think parents must understand that a medical diagnosis of autism is, of course related to seeking medical treatments, where an educational eligibility of autism is more focused on developing an educational plan with objectives and goals to help the child function in the school setting and receive special education services. For some parents, autism comes up quickly when the early childhood development specialists or speech therapists working in the home setting start to notice red flags or possible signs of autism. These specialists will start documenting these characteristics and often talk to the parents about the possibility of autism.

There are times when parents seek out medical treatment to find answers to a child's unusual behavior or restricted interests. Yet, there are parents who come through the school district as a referral from the local school or an agency or they just want answers or help for the child.

Questions to consider:
Are there major differences among professionals about the certainty of autism or do most professionals see very similar characteristics in the child?

Did professionals provide strong evidence and documentation for their reasons to go or not go with an autism eligibility or diagnosis?

Questionable Lack of Knowledge

Many times professionals have gone to certain colleges or universities where training and education is focused in one particular area. Some educational programs are so specialized with one direction or faculty that all have training in one area that college students are not exposed to the board picture of autism and how some characteristics exist along side of other medical and psychological conditions. Although the graduate students and professionals are well trained in that one area, they may have a lack of training and practical experience in identifying different delays, disorders or syndromes that may better describe a child. There may be a lack of knowledge in how medical treatments, therapies, educational strategies and medications could impact a child's communication and social skills. The professionals may lack knowledge of how an injury, a vision or hearing impairment or how numerous other conditions could impact the characteristics the child presents in a session. These graduate students and professionals do not have bad intentions, but simply don't have a wide perspective of experience and training to look at other options and possibilities than autism. When a person has a limited perspective of autism from lack of knowledge or focused training in one area, he or she may not be able to see the characteristics of autism that overlap with other conditions or disorders. As a result, important information on the child's health, behavior, social history and wellness may be overlooked or wrongly identified as autism.

Questions to consider:
Did the professionals look at other syndromes and disorders that may better describe a child's condition if autism was doubtful?

Did the professional take into consideration health conditions (i.e. injuries, prematurity, hearing and visual impairments) that impact autism characteristics or possible delays?

Questionable Autism Disorders

I once heard a person say that the term Pervasive Developmental Disorder (Not Otherwise Specified) also known as PDD-NOS was an awkward or unclear term. I think as a professional that any disorder with the (NOS) tag after it causes me to question the real specifics of the disorder. I have worked with many teams of professionals who would interpret PDD-NOS in a variety of ways. Some team members would say there are signs of autism in PDD-NOS so go with an eligibility of autism, while other team members would say it is not a clear cut diagnosis for autism and is used when the doctor is unsure if the child has autism. There are major discussions and ongoing debates in psychological circles and organizations about the use of this term and its classification in autism diagnosis and eligibilities. It makes me as a professional want to ask more questions to validate or rule out various characteristics of a disorder or syndrome. This is not an easy process as some disorders seem to be plagued with unclear criteria and general inconsistencies in understanding how a disorder presents in a child. As a parent, I would want to know why the doctor or the team went in the direction of that particular disorder. It would also be helpful to get the doctor's or team members thoughts or ideas as to why they were not specific enough to go a different direction. Many autism terms for disorders are changing, so parents and professionals must see new guidelines, state/federal standards as well as diagnostic manual changes to understand how they impact educational eligibility.

Questions to consider:
Manuals and organizations are changing terms and classifications for some autism disorders, are these changing terms and requirements being discussed with parents?

Are parents clear about what autism terms mean and how they impact a child's eligibility of autism or another condition?

Questionable Autism Descriptions

The terms and descriptors autism and autism spectrum disorder can be confusing to many in the field of autism. Sometimes autism and autism spectrum disorder are determined by test scores on certain standardized instruments. One score may suggest autism and another score may be classified as autism spectrum disorder. There are other times when some professionals and school districts simply interchange the terms autism and autism spectrum disorder and regard them as the same. There have been some changes in diagnostic manuals that school psychologists and other professionals use as they look at eligibility and diagnosis in the autism area. Some of these changes seem to focus more on autism spectrum disorder and that would be seen more as an 'umbrella term.' Therefore what would have been a separate diagnosis or eligibility in the past would be under a broader term possibly like autism spectrum disorder. I remember once seeing a school district change eligibility forms from the term autism to autism spectrum disorder, but the basic description of the disorder was the same for both terms with only minor variations. This is an example of how a school district simply interchanged the terms autism and autism spectrum disorder. I think some school districts go with Autism Spectrum Disorder as a broader and more encompassing term or descriptor to describe a child with autism characteristics. The future is still being defined in the terms and descriptors being used in the field of autism as laws and diagnostic descriptions change.

Questions to consider:
What terms or descriptors does a school district use to describe an autism eligibility or the requirements to be classified as having autism?

Do the parents understand what the professional terms or eligibility of autism mean in relation to the child's educational planning and school experience?

Questionable 'Safe' Eligibility

There are some pressures in school districts to be safe and make a quick determination and immediate autism eligibility. I think this kind of thinking is that in some school districts this might be away to avoid lawsuits. If a school district determines autism 'now' the bases are covered and then an autism eligibility can be changed if the child makes adequate progress from interventions. On the other hand, there may be some team members who question that a child may be delayed or have another condition even though the autism types of rating scales indicate some characteristics of autism. At times, professionals in clinics will note the child may have exhibited some age appropriate play skills or communication patterns and say informally that it would be better to look developmental delays. However, the school teams sometimes worry about the legal realms and are concerned if they will get sued either way. For example, a school district might be sued if they go developmental delays and the scores indicate autism. As a result, the team may go with a 'safe' autism eligibility and then exit the child if the child meets developmental milestones and makes successful academic progress. The 'safe' eligibility to avoid legal issues is not always best for the child. We can not forget as professionals that we are looking at the best interest of the child who may need different interventions or a more specialized program to address the various issues of autism and developmental delays.

Questions to consider:
Did team members get a full picture of the child to make sure the child meets the eligibility category of autism?

If there were doubts about the autism eligibility did the assessment team members document concerns and issues that need to be revisited or monitored by the school?

Questionable Autism Consultation

There are some websites on autism that emphasize a 'this or that' way approach to addressing autism concerns. This suggests that one approach is superior to all other considerations. Some websites seem to emphasize a medical approach or diagnosis to that of a school eligibility of autism. The truth is that neither the medical field or the educational field is perfect. Some medical doctors are highly trained in various aspects of autism and quite frankly other medical doctors have had very limited training in working with children with autism characteristics. On the other hand some school professionals have had more experience and training in autism than other professionals in a school district. What is probably needed is more consultation between the medical professionals diagnosing autism and the school professionals who determine educational eligibility for autism. I have seen that some doctors suggest autism concerns to the parent, then send the parent to the school district diagnostic clinic for an assessment and then ask the parent to bring the school district report back to the doctor before there is an official diagnosis of autism by the doctor. In this case, the doctor sought input from educational professionals for a broader look at the child. Consultation is encouraged in many professions, but with overloads in caseloads for both medical and educational professionals this simple communication tool could really increase professional knowledge and relationships in a way that would improve the lives of children and parents dealing with autism concerns.

Questions to consider:
Did professionals from the medical and education profession consult with any outside sources to obtain information about autism concerns for the child?

Was input obtained from professionals working with the child (e.g. home intervention specialists, preschool teachers, etc.) to gain more information about the child?

Questionable Rise of Autism

One could even question why there is a such a big rise in the number of autism cases. There could be several reasons for explaining this rise in cases. It could have been that years ago not as many people were tested for autism since they were unfamiliar with it. However, now more people are being tested and there is a rise in autism numbers. I think the media has well exposed the public to many topics related to autism. Now that autism is a highly publicized disorder there are more diagnostic centers testing and evaluating children for autism concerns. In some cases this high publicity of autism has as one of my colleagues says 'muddied the water' of autism because just the sheer mention to the word 'autism' opens the door for many clinics to immediately test for autism, even if the parent is misguided and confused about the characteristics of autism. I worked in a diagnostic center for years assessing children for developmental delays, health impairments, cognitive disabilities and autism. However, that soon changed and became a place where autism has had to be addressed numerous times in a day by many different educational professionals. It appears that perhaps years ago there were autism concerns if the child had severe deficits in communication and social skills. There is currently a broad range of children tested for autism and those with only mild symptoms of autism may receive minor or major services to address the autism concerns. As a result, a broad range of children are being identified and that has sparked a rise in autism evaluation cases.

Questions to consider:
Are autism rates going up because the field of autism has highly publicized the disorder or are these true cases of autism that should or should not be pursued?

Do some agencies only focus children's evaluations on autism to the point that other delays are overlooked?

Questionable Life Long Disability

Practically every other day I pick up a newspaper or see an online article that someone has been 'cured' from autism. What was once explained as a life long disability is now being questioned.

Although some disorders and syndromes have a stable set of signs and characteristics there is a belief by some that autism can have changing symptoms that impact the child's development and skills to interact and adapt to various people and environments. You will start hearing terms like maturing, outgrowing, fading and late development used to express these changes taking place in children who have been identified with autism and start making tremendous progress. There are many thoughts and ideas about autism and some people would even suggest that the child initially diagnosed with autism can make big changes in their growth and development or learn some new social skills. The age old questions start to be brought up and the first one is whether the child was misdiagnosed with autism or maybe he or she just had a severe speech or developmental delay? The second notion is that a change occurred and that could have been from many things like a change in diet or that the child had a good response to the interventions given at an early age. Another notion is that developmental changes are taking place within the child. Perhaps the child was severely delayed when tested, but started to blossom at a later age. Finally, one cannot leave out the fact that a different diagnosis may actually better describe the child than autism.

Questions to consider:
Does my child exhibit the characteristics of autism on a daily basis or is there evidence that he or she may be responding well to interventions and need a different program?

Should my child be reassessed and evaluated again if major changes are occurring in the child's communication patterns and social interaction skills?

Questionable Professional Observation

There are times when professionals see different things in the child and that causes a parent to question if a child has autism or is delayed in areas such as social interaction, restricted interests and communication. Professional observations can focus on different areas such as nursing, speech therapy, occupational therapy, physical therapy, vision and hearing fields and school psychology. For example, a child who tantrums and is rebellious may be observed in different ways by professionals who have had different training and educational experiences. The nurse may notice the child exhibited purposeful behavior as he said 'no' and then turned to look at his parents for approval or disapproval almost appearing as a child with a social delay. A speech therapist may notice the same child's high pitched vocalizations and a child running away with no awareness of his social surroundings as sending up red flags for autism consideration. A school psychologist may notice the child has tantrums when given direct assessment tasks, but plays appropriately in free play when no demands are placed on him or her. Professionals on a team with differing points of view can be a strength in educating team members about the various aspects of autism, but they may also cause big conflicts and place doubt in the parent's view of a possible diagnosis or eligibility. The differing professional observations may cause the parent to question an autism possibility or consideration. Parents are trying to take this information and put it in perspective to what they know and have experienced with the child.

Questions to consider:

Did the professionals take time to discuss their observations with the parent during or after the assessment?

Were the professional's observations documented in an educational eligibility report or in a doctor's medical report and or records?

Questionable Inconsistent Information

Sometimes parents will hear inconsistent information from professionals regarding autism. A parent may hear phrases like 'possibly autism,' 'he's on the borderline for autism,' 'maybe he has autism' or 'she even has some characteristics of autism.' This is confusing to parents who then become unsure if the child has autism because of the inconsistent information. There are times when a parent may interpret these uncertainties as a sign that his or her child does some things appropriately and other things inappropriately. The parent then has the opportunity to question professionals about the broad range of behaviors and then get more specific information regarding the child's behavior, social interactions and communication patterns. If parents are unfamiliar with terms they made need to ask professionals for clarification, take notes and look up terms on the internet, in a library or consult with other parents to understand the specifics of the child's behavior. Parents are searching for definite answers and sometimes the answers to some questions are not clear and precise and parents find conflicting and confusing information. New information on autism is coming out daily for both professionals and parents and each new idea seems to bring up more questions and more issues. Some of the information on autism is more user friendly and helpful to parents as they wade through lots of information, while other articles are more complex and confusing for parents and professionals.

Questions to consider:
What are the specific behaviors and characteristics that make the professional question whether the child has autism?

Are there any specific concerns that might cast doubt on whether or not my child has autism or another condition?

Chapter 3
Questionable Autism Parenting Issues

Parents have many questions on issues dealing with the topic of autism. These issues can spread from a questionable family history of autism to making pressured decisions about an educational autism eligibility. There are times when parents have some knowledge of the topic of autism, avoid the idea of autism or just justify for or against an autism diagnosis or eligibility. Parents may start to question the progress the child is making in the school environment. Issues related to the change of school settings and how it may impact a child are discussed as well as how it may be an indicator of some autistic or delayed characteristics. It is hoped that exploring some of these parent issues will generate new questions in the area of autism.

The chapter also explores some other issues related to autism that parents may face. Parents may have varying degrees of knowledge about autism and start to justify the child's behaviors and actions from different angles. As well, parent issues related to immaturity issues, sensory issues and delays are discussed in relation to autism. There is a look at over cueing children and prompting only with a cue. The chapter includes a discussion of child phrases that sometimes parents don't see or notice as unusual or different. For instance, there are examples of child phrases that appear typical at first, but are really more rote types of phrases that the child may use on a daily basis as a routine or memorized type of phrase. Parents have many concerns, issues and questions that need to be explored and see how these issues may be questionable in understanding whether their children may have autism and or other types of delays, conditions, syndromes or disorders.

Questionable Family History of Autism

Sometimes a parent will naturally assume that a child has autism because the sibling has a diagnosis of autism. Although, siblings of a child with autism can certainly have autism, not every sibling has autism just because a brother or sister has it. One reason a parent might automatically assume a younger child has autism is because the young child may start mimicking or imitating the behaviors of an older child with autism so the younger child may appear to almost have some autism characteristics. A parent may suggest that a child does not respond to a social greeting. On observation, the school psychologist walks through the office and waves 'bye' to the child. The child does not respond immediately, but a few minutes later turns and waves at the school psychologist through a glass window. It is important to note that in most cases the staff has not seen the other child and do not know for sure if a brother or sister has a correct diagnosis or a misdiagnosis of autism. The child coming in to be assessed may show no signs of autism at all. Going down the hallway at the assessment the child could be interactive, pointing to objects and making eye contact when approached by the staff. The child may make attempts to communicate by showing an interest in others. He or she could reach out to parents and others for toys in the testing room. This is one of those examples of 'no symptoms,' but 'I think the child has autism.' Autism is a word people have started to use more frequently to describe many behaviors that may cross over to other areas of delays, conditions and syndromes.

Questions to consider:

What characteristics did the child exhibit that indicated autism or possible autism concerns?

Did the child make communication efforts to socially interact with the parent or professionals working with the child?

Questionable Justification of Behaviors

It is not uncommon for parents to justify or downplay autism behaviors or characteristics because they want everything to be 'ok.' The parent wants to think the child's actions are just a normal part of development so he or she tries to justify that it is 'ok' to do various things. For example, as professionals arrive for a home visit the front door is opened and the child takes off and runs down the street to avoid social contact. Instead of trying to stop the child and redirect the child to a safer activity the parent may justify the child's action of running down the street as if it were 'ok.' A parent may say 'its ok, he is just taking a sensory break and just needs to release his energy.' There are times when some parents have just become accustomed to the child's unusual behaviors so it seems acceptable to the family who is familiar with the child. However, when other people start commenting that the child has really unusual patterns of behavior or communicates in a very limited way then concerns are brought out. Some parents may need to be refocused to recognize that these may be strong signals or characteristics of autism. If sensory breaks are repetitive or ritualistic (e.g. needing to run back and forth in the hallway many times during a short period or turning the lights on and off repeatedly) then there are concerns that the child may have some autistic characteristics. The different types of behaviors may need to be discussed with the parent to gain an understanding of the relationship to autism and behaviors.

Questions to consider:

Does the parent understand how the child's behaviors or restricted interests relate to autism concerns?

Did the professional help explain to the parent any unusual behaviors the child exhibits that are related to autism?

Questionable Autism Knowledge

Some parents have studied the internet and read up on autism so they know the buzz words to justify or ignore the child's behaviors. Sometimes this autism knowledge is used to explain the child's behavior, but at other times it is used to make excuses and avoid talking about the child's true concerns. We have all heard the old saying about a little knowledge being very dangerous and this is sometimes the case with autism information. If a child runs to another room to avoid social interaction with a developmental specialist, speech therapist or school psychologist during a home visit the parent may have a well thought out explanation. A parent may say 'he is just taking a personal time out and when he is ready he will come back in the room.' Basically the parent has a justification for each action of the child as a way to redirect attention from the child's withdrawal or avoidance types of behavior. Observations by professionals need to be specific and detailed to help parents clarify the child's behaviors and actions in a way to help parents see a new angle or gain more knowledge about autism. There are also times when parents focus on one aspect of autism that they have learned and base their ideas about autism on a particular article, person or approach. The parent views the child's condition just from one angle and may need help generalizing a broader picture adding new information to his or her perspective about autism.

Questions to consider:
Does the parent understand the broad aspects of autism or is there a very limited and specific belief about autism?

What are some ways to educate parents so they can gain more knowledge about autism and broaden their perspectives about autism?

Questionable Change of Setting

It is not uncommon for parents to request a child with autism be exited from a program because the child has made tremendous progress in one setting or grade level. Sometimes a parent may notice a child is doing very well in the lower grades like first or second grade where some of the information used is rote learning and memorization. When the parent sees the child's wonderful ability to retain simple facts and general knowledge he or she may request a child to be exited from an autism program. However, things may change in the upper grades when the child is asked to make conclusions and clarify or explain information related to classroom topics. The child may begin to struggle in the upper grades and still need special education support. This can also be seen in a change of schools like moving from elementary school to a large middle school. Sometimes children with autism may cope really well in the smaller more confined setting of an elementary school where supports are in place and readily available to help the child. The parent may be so proud of the child that he or she requests a quick exit from special education. However, middle school often brings about a bigger, less structured setting. Some students with autism are expected to be more independent and can be caught in a situation with less support and more challenges. The child with autism may not understand the humor, joking, gentle teasing and social meanings coming toward him or her at a fast pace.

Questions to consider:
Did parents and professionals look at the changing support a child may need as a child goes to a new school setting or makes a grade level change?

Are supports in place for a child changing a school setting and has there been contact with staff to discuss the particular issues and concerns of the child coming to the new school?

Questionable Immaturity Issues

There are also incidents where a parent chalks autism concerns up as immaturity issues for the child. The parent may falsely feel if the child spends an extra year in daycare or preschool the unusual behaviors will go away. There is sometimes the perception that the child will 'grow out' of the naughty or tantrum behaviors if he or she will just take another year of preschool and learn how to control him or herself. It is not that another year of preschool may help (or not help) the child, but rather looking at the child to see if immaturity is the issue or is this a child with major deficits in communication, social interaction and restricted types of interests. Sometimes it is tricky and takes another professional to spot unusual characteristics or lack of responses from the child. Some parents use this 'immaturity issues' argument to justify a child's actions who is not using speech. The parent may be convinced the child is just 'shy and immature' and once he or she gets around other children the child will learn to have conversations with others. A parent may feel the child just lacks general social interaction skills and needs 'to learn to make friends.' Professionals often have to work with the parents to question if 'immaturity' is the real issue or if autism or other behavioral issues are standing out. Professionals and parents may explore 'immaturity' versus a child who is extremely isolated, withdrawn or totally in a solitary type of play where he or she may lack total awareness of other children around him or her.

Questions to consider:
Is the child displaying strong characteristics of autism or are there issues of immaturity that are obvious in the child's behaviors and actions?

Does the child make attempts to communicate with others in social interaction settings or does the child just lack skills in understanding how to communicate with others?

Questionable Sensory Issues

Not every child with autism has sensory issues. The same is also true in that not all children with sensory issues have autism. Sensory issues can take many forms as some children are just awkward and weak in how the motor and sensory skills connect. Sensory issues may also be related to cultural experiences. A child taking his or her shoes off to feel the texture of the carpet may be different than a child taking his or her shoes off because everyone in the household takes shoes off upon entering the house. Some children seem to over-respond to various sensory related activities. For example, some children may have strong reactions to lightness or darkness or possibly the sound of a toy or fire alarm. The other side of the issue is that some children may show hardly any reaction or really under-respond to a sensory experience. I had a parent share that her son was so withdrawn that he would not react to a fire alarm. She noted that a loud noise or sound would get absolutely no reaction from her son at all. This was not unusual because this was a child who was so withdrawn that many things could be happening around the young boy at one time and he was totally unaware of the social interactions and communication taking place in a social environment. Sensory issues can be one characteristic of autism, but they are also part of a larger picture that involves the child's communication, social interaction, interests and behavior issues.

Questions to consider:
Does the child's sensory awareness issues impact his or her communication, social interactions and interests?

Are the child's sensory issues related to cultural experiences or home traditions rather than difficulties with exploration in the environment?

Questionable Delays

A parent or guardian may notice that a child doesn't seem quite right or there is a feeling the child has some type of delay. Sometimes these are legitimate concerns and at other times there is just some confusion about typical development in children. There are times when a parent feels if a child does not know everything the child must be delayed or have autism. Sometimes the parents expectations for school readiness are skewed because they want the child to go to medical school in the future and expect the child to be able to complete many educational tasks at an early age. At other times, parents may be comparing a child with a sibling. There have been occasions where a parent will compare a younger child with a gifted sibling, so the younger child looks extremely delayed because he or she is being compared to a child with cognitive abilities in the advanced or bright range. However, when the younger child is tested it may reveal the child is in the average range for his or her cognitive abilities when compared to other same age kids. As well, autism may not even be an issue if the child interacted appropriately during the assessment and with others throughout the assessment. If the parent is unsure where the child falls in relation to delays, there are many resources to help. There is usually information published about how the child is reaching certain milestones in his or her development. Various early diagnostic centers will assess children to see if the child is on target in his or her development or has delays or autism concerns.

Questions to consider:
What possible signs of autism does my child show that stand out or present in his or her social interaction and communication with others?

Does the child have some delays that are red flags for possible autism concerns that should be evaluated?

Questionable Over Cueing

There have been a few situations related to autism where I noticed that the parent was over cueing the child. This can easily happen as the parent is trying to help guide and teach the child. Sometimes the parent will say something like 'show mommy the ....' or a similar phrase and the child only does the task when given the cue. I have heard parents say the child will only pick up toys if the 'clean up song' is presented. The first thing that happens in a classroom is when a substitute or different teacher makes a cleanup request without singing the 'clean up song.' The perfect cue was not given and now the question is how the child will respond when a different cue or person gives a request. The person who lacks training may first think the child is responding very positively to the cue and the request was accomplished as desired. However, another professional may see that a cue has to presented for every single request or action that the child completes. As a result, the child is limited in social interactions and only shares information in a limited social context with specific cues. The goal of many educational professionals is to help the child generalize skills to different situations and people. Over cueing may prevent this generalization because there is a tendency to teach the child that everything is done in a certain way with a specific cue. The child will only complete the tasks or requests if it is given with a prompt or specific cue from a certain person or in a certain situation.

Questions to consider:
Will the child complete a task or request when it is not given with a cue or prompt from a specific person?

What are some ways to help a child complete the same task when a request is given by a different person in a different situation?

Questionable Child Phrases

There are times when parents hear a child say phrases that almost sound interactive, but these statements are actually rote types of phrases. The child might have just repeated phrases again and again so sometimes the phrases are used in appropriate situations and at other times parents start to notice that the child says a certain phrase in an inappropriate situation or says the same word for everything. I often hear parents say that a child may use the word 'no' for everything, even if the child wants the ice cream cone or brand new toy. This is showing that the child lacks an understanding of the meaning behind the word or phrase. One rote type of phrase would be greetings such as 'nice to meet you,' 'love you' or 'how are you?' So many times these sound like appropriate greetings, but there is usually no more interaction after the child gives the greeting. Another type of phrase would be possession phrases like 'no, mine,' 'it's mine,' or "I want it' and these are repeated many times. Congratulatory phrases such as 'you did it' or 'good job' seem nice on the surface, but after a while they just sound repetitive and less meaningful. The old question phrase can often be repeated thousands of times as the child continually says 'what's that' even though it has been explained to the child numerous times. There are also rote phrases that are used to gain attention like 'mommy look,' 'want more,' or the child that says 'that's what I am talking about' over and over again.

Questions to consider:
Is the child using the phrase to communicate intent or is child using the phrase as a repetitive saying?

Is the child's word or phrase being said in a practical way of communicating versus a phrase that lacks meaning or is used inappropriately?

Questionable Pressured Decision

One thing that happens in the special education process is that often parents are expected to make important decisions related to autism with quick or somewhat pressured responses. The parents bring the child in for the assessment and then usually several weeks (or maybe a month) later they come to the school district for an eligibility meeting. The team who assessed the child will go over the results and tell the parent if the child is eligible for special education services or that the child is not eligible for services. Sometimes parents feel like they are bombarded with too much information at these meetings. I have heard parents say things like 'I need more time to study this' or 'I need to talk to my husband about this.' Following the eligibility meeting the parents are often asked if they want services and then they are asked to sign a form that they agree for the team to develop an educational plan for the child. This is often done as a continuation of the eligibility meeting that the parent has just completed. Parents are usually told this is a starting point and they can always op-out or discontinue services or request a meeting at the school to make changes in the plan. The process is informative and helpful for parents as it is usually packed with lots of information about the child. However, the downside is that parents don't have a lot of time to reflect on these decisions and may feel pressure to make a decision for the child 'right now.' This process of a quick decision is a little uncomfortable for some parents.

Questions to consider:
Did the assessment team check with the parent to make sure he or she had a good understanding of the testing results and decisions related to autism or other concerns?

Do the parents understand that they can initiate and request changes if the plan is not meeting the child's needs?

Chapter 4
Questionable Autism Practices

Chapter four spans wide with a discussion of many practices or real world experiences related to autism. Certainly understanding a program's philosophy or an agency's approach would help a person explore the program or agency's view of autism and how they work with children. The topic of confusion related to disorders, autism symptoms and differing philosophical views is explored. The chapter also looks at autism related to communicating autism placement changes in a school setting. There are also other topics considered such as the parent who questions autism when the child is really lacking in certain skills.

The chapter continues with a look at observable behaviors in relation to other conditions or syndromes. It helps to have an understanding that different professionals may observe behaviors from varying perspectives. A nurse might view an observational behavior from a medical perspective where a teacher may view the same behavior related to an educational or classroom perspective. Other topics considered are related to support and educational planning when a child has symptoms of autism. This support can vary from family support to individual support of the child or a combination of both. In addition, the topic of intervention is explored in relation to the length of time a young child has received or not received early intervention services. The issues related to the real world autism practices cover a variety issues that parents and professionals face everyday. Theses practical issues can impact how an agency or program views a child as well as the services and support the child receives.

Questionable Program Philosophy

A program or agency can vary in a certain type of philosophy on autism. For example, if a program has a philosophy of 'rule in or rule out' autism after one assessment that can put pressure on the professionals to make an eligibility decision quickly. This may work fine in cases with clear cut symptoms of autism that are obvious or in a child that doesn't show any characteristics of autism. However, on cases where the child is showing some appropriate communication and social interaction skills along with some inconsistent or limited behaviors then more information or observations may be needed. Other programs may use a 'tie breaker' method to determine an autism eligibility. For instance one autism type of checklist may have a 'possibly' range and another instrument may show a very likely type of possibility of autism. A team may decide to use another instrument and conduct a home observation to obtain more information on the child's behavior. This home assessment and observation is sometimes the 'tie breaker' to determine if a team will go eligible or non-eligible for an autism eligibility. However, professionals can vary in their approach and how much information they obtain from a home assessment. These are the times I wish these programs or agencies would not jump into an immediate eligibility of autism. My dream would be to see a temporary classroom program for six to eight weeks to gather more observations on the child before making an autism determination when there are questions or uncertainties.

Questions to consider:
Were the signs and symptoms of autism obvious in the child or were there major questions about how the child responded in the assessment?

Did the professionals use a lot of terms such as 'limited,' 'inconsistent' or 'uncertain' to describe the child's behavior, interaction or communication?

Questionable Autism Agency Approaches

Sometimes a parent will deal with community agencies and school districts in different ways. For example, a parent that is in denial about autism concerns may simply tell an agency (working with various children up to age 2 and a half) that he or she doesn't want to pursue autism concerns at this time. The agency may or may not accept the parent's refusal of an evaluation or any other types of assessment that was planned for the child. However, when the child comes into many school districts the approach to an issue about autism may be different. The school district is required to evaluate the child when there is a suspected disability of autism. The parent then has to make a decision if they want to pursue the school district's assessment for autism or refuse services to complete the assessment. It would be just an incomplete evaluation if the parent decides not to complete testing for the child. Professionals may need to spend more time with parents to explain the importance of the assessment and the information it will provide them. It is important to note that a school district is making a determination about autism from an educational perspective and not from a medical treatment approach. The school district is trying to determine the type of special education services and best type of placement for the child's educational needs related to autism and other educational types of disabilities. Therefore, parents need to decide if they want to complete the full assessment for the child or have an incomplete assessment for autism.

Questions to consider:
Was a full autism assessment completed on the child or were parts of the assessment refused by the parent?

Was an explanation given to the parents about why autism concerns need to be addressed and how the testing instruments or checklists could be valuable in determining autism?

Questionable Confusion about Disorders

A confusing aspect for many parents is that some autism symptoms are also the same characteristics for other disorders or developmental delays. The parent may only be familiar with various traits of autism so other disorders or delays are not even considered. Some parents will question the whole idea of autism and say the child just has 'a few delays.' The reason most eligibility teams don't give a child an eligibility of autism and developmental delays together is that delays are part of autism. The autism eligibility form usually indicates that autism can cause either developmental delays or show patterns of uneven skill development. The autism eligibility form also may indicate to a greater degree that the child has deficits related to communication difficulties, social skills, restricted interests and sensory issues. However, for some parents all this information about delays mixed in with autism is confusing for some parents. For example, a child who throws tantrums can be viewed as having characteristics of autism. However, throwing tantrums can also be present in children with behavioral issues such as hyperactivity or children who experience depression, anxiety or aggression. A full medical, social and behavioral family history may provide more answers to some of these other conditions or disorders. Therefore, the parents need to look at the broad picture of how traits or behaviors represent the concerns of the child in relation to autism as well as other disorders that may better describe the child.

Questions to consider:
Are the symptoms of the child and information from the family medical and social history leaning toward other conditions that better describe the child than autism?

Did the parent consult with professionals about doubts, concerns or strong feelings related to an autism eligibility or consideration?

Questionable Skills that are Lacking

There are times when parents suspect a child has autism because he or she is lacking the skills in a certain area. Skill levels can be lacking in a broad range of areas. A child could lack skills and have minor delays in one area like speech and communication, while some other children lack skills and have delays in many different areas. There are also children who have significant or major delays that impact their skill development and who may need intensive interventions and support. Some children with a very severe speech and language impairment may present with similar characteristics of a child with autism. It takes a knowledgeable professional to recognize if the child has the potential to communicate with others, but may be lacking the skills to be able to effectively communicate with others. For instance, a child who is not using words to express him or herself may be seen by the parent as a child with autism. However, professionals observing the child may view the child in a broader way. The child could have a limited vocabulary and need more experiences to expand his or her vocabulary and use of words. The child may be gesturing for items and not using words to request items because he or she lacks the words to describe his or her wants or needs. One person may view the child as having autism and another person may see the child as lacking communication skills, social interaction experiences or has had a lack of opportunity to develop skills.

Questions to consider:

Does the child have an autism trait because he or she has had a lack of opportunity to develop a skill?

Is the child presenting with other delays that are related to a lack of skills that better describe him or her than autism?

Questionable Support and Planning

I know that some professionals lump autism into one category, but treatment and educational planning will vary with the severity of symptoms and needs of the child. As well, support for the needs of the child is also an issue. At times you will hear some organizations say they support the needs of the family and this mission is good when the family supports the child's needs. However, when the families' wants and needs (e.g. wanting a full day program for child care convenience rather than a half day recommended program) interfere with what is best for the child there can be problems. For example, some children with autism characteristics will need more intensive interventions and classroom adaptations, while other children may function with minor adjustments in the classroom. Parents must question if these adaptations, interventions or strategies are working for the child or not and then consult with the school professionals for support and planning. The parents and professionals may need to look at the child's abilities and skills to see where adjustments can be made in the school or classroom settings. The multidisciplinary team at the school may need to meet and discuss if the child has had regression in skills or significant deficits that need to be addressed. On the other hand, if the child has responded positively to interventions then a less restrictive learning environment or class may be considered in planning the child's education.

Questions to consider:
Were different levels of support considered to help the child adapt to a new school or classroom setting?

Are the child's needs given full consideration when looking at placement for an autism eligibility in a school or home setting?

Questionable Intervention Time

The concept that young children have received early intervention is one that can be questioned. Some states have long waiting lists to be assessed for early childhood intervention and pre-school programs. There is quite a variability among agencies in that some children have received interventions from infancy and other children have had no early intervention services at all. As a school psychologist, when I am assessing a child for autism concerns and developmental delays, I like to find out information on the child's intervention history. I would question the parent to find out if the child had received any early intervention services. I may need to ask if the child had home visits from professionals to work with him or her or if the child attended a play group or head start type of program. I would look to see if the child qualified for early intervention services, but the parents chose not to participate for a variety of reasons (e.g. moved, job difficulties or work settings or simply difficulty in scheduling). I might see if the child qualified for services, but was placed on a waiting list to receive the services at a later time. I also want to see if the child has attended a structured preschool or daycare program and how the child responded in this setting. It is getting a picture of a child to see if the child has had intervention services for several years and what his or her response was to the services versus a child who has had no interventions at all.

Questions to consider:

What was the length of time and the type of intervention services (e.g. speech and language services, developmental specialist, behavioral specialist, etc.) the child received?

Was the child evaluated to receive early intervention services and did the child receive any services after that evaluation?

Questionable Autism Philosophy

There are certainly different philosophical views about considering autism so this is confusing for both parents and professionals. For instance, some professionals may note red flags or possible autism, but choose to take a 'wait and see' approach. These professionals may want to watch the child a little more after the child has had some interventions before making a definitive diagnosis or autism eligibility. There are certainly some philosophies that don't want to beat around the bush and suggest that a thorough assessment be completed in order to 'rule in or rule out' autism before the interventions start. Yet other programs are convinced that a variety of therapies or approaches (e.g. regulated or special diets, possible medications, holistic supplements, vitamins and an array or therapies) should be tried before autism and behavioral concerns need to be addressed more specifically. Not only do professionals have varying opinions in how they want to start addressing the child's autism concerns, but many parents have different philosophical approaches. Some parents want to turn their heads and hope the autism concerns will go away or be less of a burden on the family. Other parents are very proactive and want to address all autism concerns head on, while other parents are more relaxed and prefer to take a back seat until autism concerns just have to be addressed. There is quite a range of autism philosophies so sometimes conflicts arise, while at other times it is agreeable.

Questions to consider:
Do the parents and the program have similar philosophies about the approach to address the child's autism concerns?

What are some ways parents and professionals can work out their disagreements when they have philosophical differences related to autism concerns?

Questionable Change in Autism Placement

Sometimes professionals will write in a report that a child is currently receiving special education services in the area of autism. There are times when this information is inaccurate. For example, child may have been misdiagnosed with autism and a diagnosis or educational eligibility has changed. A child may have been exited from an autism program and placed in a regular education program with no special education support. However, when educational records are not updated in the schools, information that is incorrect is continually passed on through a school system. Busy educational professionals may overlook or miss that there has been a change in the child's placement or eligibility. Parents who are more familiar with the child's educational journey can provide valuable input about the child's educational placement.

A parent may not catch all of the details during a long special education meeting when lots of information is given to him or her. However, parents can sometimes be unaware of or lack an understanding of placement or eligibility changes. Parents are given a mountain of paperwork in the special education process and sometimes parents may miss details in a change of placement. If there are language barriers the autism placement change can be even more confusing as a parent may need to wait months for a translated copy of a report in backed up school districts. It is really important to adequately communicate autism placement changes to parents and professionals.

Questions to consider:
Are the child's school records and testing information current in the child's school folder and is that information available to professionals working with the child and the parent?

Were changes in eligibility or placement updated, corrected or revised in the child's school enrollment information?

Questionable Symptom Confusion

There are sometimes autism concerns that confuse parents about the possible symptoms of autism. Let's take for example that sometimes a withdrawn child presents with symptoms of autism. This child may by totally unaware of his or her environment or dangerous situations that are in the home, school or community. This is somewhat different from a child who is withdrawn and has behavioral issues. A young child presenting with socialization delays may choose to become more withdrawn at times. An example would be a parent describing a child who plays with other children in a preschool setting for about ten minutes and then goes off and plays by himself and doesn't want anything else to do with the other children. In this case the child is attempting to avoid communicating and playing with other children and therefore the withdrawal behavior becomes somewhat purposeful. Another example could be related to a child who is not using words. Some children with autism may be so withdrawn that they never speak or use language to communicate a concern, request or need. This example is quite different from a child choosing not to speak to gain attention, get his or her way or gain control of a situation. Some children don't speak because they are being waited on hand and foot by an older sibling so the need to use communication is not necessary. The intent is usually not there for children with autism concerns, but is quite obvious in children with behavioral and socialization issues.

Questions to consider:
Is the child's possible autism characteristics presented with purposeful intent with some type of attempt to communicate needs and wants to another person?

Did the professionals observe the child in a variety of settings with various objects to see if the child shows a desire or makes an attempt to reach out to another person?

Questionable Observable Behaviors

There are times when parents report numerous behaviors related to autism characteristics, but the professionals don't see those behaviors at all or see the behaviors connected to other concerns. Sometimes professionals must educate parents on other possible explanations for characteristics or behaviors that may appear similar to autism. A nursing professional may review health conditions such as prematurity, prenatal drug and alcohol abuse and what impact that can have on a child's activity level. As well, a school psychologist can review the social and behavioral history of the child and family to see if other conditions present with similar characteristics of autism. Sometimes conditions such as ADHD, various processing disorders, an array of emotional disorders, cognitive and speech impairments may trigger and resemble some similar behaviors and traits as children with autism. This is an area that may need considerable explanation to the parent as some parents may only be familiar with the characteristics of autism because it is a highly publicized disorder. These parents are probably totally unaware that many other conditions and especially developmental delays can appear with some similar characteristics of autism. I think professionals must take the time to explore the other possibilities that could be considered before an autism eligibility is immediately considered with the parent. Specific examples of the child's language, requests, behaviors and actions may need to be pointed out to the parents as observable behaviors.

Questions to consider:
Does the family medical and behavioral history mention any conditions that may have similar characteristics of autism?

Are there any other conditions or syndromes that better describe the child's overall profile than autism?

Chapter 5
Questionable Autism Research Links

Autism research spans a broad range of topics and interests. For example, it is sometimes explored as a genetic condition or from a brain or neurodevelopment perspective. This chapter includes a discussion of autism increases as well as how autism can be complicated with multiple symptoms and causes explored. There are discussions about professionals having very distinct views about autism and even how researchers disagree on the causes of autism. The questions continue in understanding autism improvement in a child with regards to interventions and developmental changes. There is an examination of how parents may have misunderstandings about the signs and symptoms of autism or read a characteristic of autism in a different way than a professional. This topic is certainly open for discussion.

The chapter explores how research areas of autism are now studied by a wide variety of people with broad research interests on the topic. As autism has impacted many families in one way or another, the interest in researching autism has spread rapidly. It has not only become an educational endeavor to find out about autism, but it has become a very personal issue for families and researchers so they can help their children, friends and family members. With the wide variety of training of the these professionals the research on autism can be both fascinating and insightful as it provides some explanations into a number of links and connected interests to the topic of autism. As professionals use different research methods and a variety of techniques to understand autism the research is seen not only as insightful, but controversial as well.

Questionable Genetic Condition

It is not uncommon for a parent to come to an early childhood diagnostic clinic with several conditions noted by a doctor. In some cases, autism comes up from the parent as the primary concern. However, after the school nurse reviews the doctor's report there may be overtones of other syndromes and medical conditions that may mimic some of the same characteristics of autism. Often times, a genetic referral packet is initiated with the parent to probe deeper into the child's genetic background. It is very possible that the young child can have one or more types of genetic conditions or syndromes that better describe his or her condition than autism. Professionals need to conduct a complete review with the parent to obtain the child's medical history when there are concerns about a possible genetic condition that surfaces with autism concerns. There is both a pro and a con of getting a genetic evaluation. The con of this is that there are only a few professionals qualified to conduct genetic evaluations and there can be long waiting lists before the child ever receives a genetic evaluation. A school team will probably be making an educational eligibility determination long before a parent receives the results of the child's genetic evaluation. The pro is that the information a parent receives from a genetic evaluation is wonderful and very detailed in finding out if there is another syndrome that better describes the concerns of the child.

Questions to consider:
Who should make the determination for a genetic referral if there are additional concerns other than autism?

How could the information from a genetic evaluation benefit a team of professionals looking at autism?

Questionable Neurodevelopment Concerns

Parents sometimes go into a panic mode when they hear the child has autism and the doctor calls it a 'neurodevelopment disorder.' This is a medical term and neurodevelopment is often called a brain development disorder or impairment. Just because a doctor says 'neurodevelopmental' does not mean the child automatically needs extensive brain scans and an intensive program. A neurodevelopmental disorder is really a much broader term and includes many other disorders than autism. In fact, many parents are unaware that ADHD is a very common neurodevelopment disorder. Most parents would say we don't need a brain scan for ADHD, we just want to get the child help in getting organized and focused more on school studies. Some parents may seek medical care or work with the school on strategies to help the child. Children with neurodevelopmental disorders are not all impacted the same. Some children with autism will need more support and have a greater degree of difficulty functioning in school and life in general, while other children will need less support. Some children with autism concerns will struggle more with intellectual issues, emotional concerns, communication issues or motor difficulties than other children. Parents may need to work with the school staff and look at effective strategies to meet the child's needs in a particular school. Programs for children with autism run the range of intensive to a regular education environment with limited support.

Questions to consider:
How is autism impacting the child's school life (academics, social friendships at school and behavior) and home life (family relationships, household tasks and family guidelines)?

What are some classroom strategies that could help a child with autism concerns function more effectively in the school setting?

Questionable Multiple Categories

The most common diagnostic mistakes seem to come from complicated information related to multiple symptoms and a variety of possible causes. This is what makes autism a more complex diagnosis or eligibility to consider. The difficulty comes from having one or several symptoms that could be autism, but may equally fall under another eligibility category or some other disorder. Sometimes a diagnosis or eligibility is questionable because a professional takes an easy approach or explanation. The professional might say 'let's just call it anxiety or a stress disorder' to avoid addressing the communication or social skills areas of a child with autism.

There are times when a foster parent or temporary guardian takes the child to the doctor and has to say that much of the birth and family history information is 'unknown.' Later the family may learn additional information related to family mental illness, school learning problems, alcohol or drug exposure and special education issues. When this additional information is noted it can quickly change a child's diagnosis or eligibility or open the door to look at different eligibility categories that may describe the child better than autism. Another point to note is that a foster parent may be unaware of whether the child has had interventions, therapy or treatment and may not be able to report if the child had intensive interventions or no interventions at all. This information would be important in helping to determine educational eligibility or the possible cause of a disorder.

Questions to consider:
Are the symptoms very specific to autism or is there concern that other disorders should possibly be considered?

Were the parents or guardians specific and detailed in sharing the difficulties or problem areas for the child or was information left out or missed in the evaluation?

Questionable Publicity Link to Autism Increases

Every day I pick up the paper or read on the internet that more and more children have autism. It is not uncommon to see that the cases of autism are increasing, so it makes me question the reasons for that increase. At first, I was thinking that autism was just the newest 'hot' disorder that many people think they have. Is it going to be like ADHD was a few years ago where everyone in the teacher's lounge shouts 'I have ADHD' at the first sign of disorganization. Could it be that autism organizations are some of the most vocal and highly publicized organizations that put a lot more information out than other childhood disorder organizations? Therefore, parents feel their children have some of these characteristics so parents are actually pursuing the autism diagnosis or eligibility. Sometimes there is a suggestion that there are changing definitions from organizations and psychological manuals that expand who qualifies for an autism eligibility or diagnosis and as a result the number of children with autism keeps growing bigger and bigger. One could even argue that the increase stems from possibly moving around labels from other types of disorders into the autism categories or just shifting special education categories around so more children fall into the autism category. For example, a child with a speech and language impairment may have been incorrectly placed under an autism educational eligibility category so that would be an increase in autism numbers from that incorrect autism eligibility.

Questions to consider:
Is the increase in autism numbers related to the amount of publicity on autism or some other factor in society?

Is there a way to screen children more effectively to determine if autism is the concern that needs to be addressed or if it does not need to be addressed?

Questionable Causes of Autism

It is incredibly difficult to state any firm fact regarding the cause of autism. There are some professionals and researchers who have very distinct ideas about autism and who are unwilling to listen to other professionals who have different ideas about autism. Basically, there is not a unified answer from professionals for the cause of autism. Some researchers seem to think it is a combination of genetic and environmental factors why other researchers disagree. The question is 'does there have to be an exact cause' of autism? Perhaps autism is like the medical condition of lupus where the cause is complex and uncertain. People seem to be 'ok' with the idea that there is not an exact cause of lupus and that they just want to treat it. Perhaps the world of autism should learn from other types of medical conditions that the exact cause of an illness or disorder may never be known. The question may even linger as to whether it is more important to know the cause of autism or is it more important to just understand the signs and symptoms of autism and then treat them through therapies and educational strategies to help the child. After all, if the child has major deficits in communication skills and social interaction with other children, could interventions and educational strategies be put into place to help children work on the specific areas they need help to develop age appropriate skills. In the same way, if a child has restricted interests then various strategies could be used to expand the child's interest in a particular topic.

Questions to consider:
Even though the cause of autism is unknown are there some key issues that stand out stronger for a possible relationship to autism?

How can professionals explain the links of autism to parents in an easy to understand and simplified way?

Questionable Autism Improvement

Many people describe autism as a lifelong disorder, but others are challenging this if they see marked improvements in a child's behavior and communication. There are varied reasons why a child may show improvement related to communication, social interaction and other autism characteristics. The first and most talked about one is that the child often has had early intervention services and responded well to the early childhood developmental specialists and speech therapists working with him or her. This improvement may have helped the child adjust better in the school setting. Another reason for childhood changes is simply that children develop at different times. You may have heard the comparison that children are like flowers and they bloom at different times. Some children bloom earlier while other children bloom or change at a later age. Other professionals seem to suggest that the brain is still developing in a child with autism and this may account for the change in skills. Many children are diagnosed or received an educational eligibility for autism before the age of three so many skills have not developed or materialized. As the child grows and develops various autism characteristics may lessen or are not as defined as they were in the very young child. This marked improvement may cause parents and professionals to wonder whether the child's improvement is only in one particular area or across the board in relation to autism improvement.

Questions to consider:
Is the child responding well from early interventions so that autism symptoms are improving?

Is the child only making marked improvement in one area or are there other areas that need to be addressed in relation to autism concerns?

Questionable Brain Research

Parents and professionals are often confused by all the different things they are hearing about brain research because not only is the field of autism complex, but the areas of brain research are even more difficult and confusing for the general public to understand. You would think the answers about autism and brain research would be simple, but think again. Brain research on autism is as varied as other types of research trying to find the 'golden answer' to autism. There has been speculation that autism is related to the size of the brain, the matter or tissue in the brain, how brain messages travel to certain regions or parts of the brain and how the brain is connected or wired. There have been considerations of brain timing issues where the child may have off beat timing concerns and the child with autism may not catch social or communication cues. However, sometimes brain research does not always present consistent results for children with autism. Because autism is a 'spectrum' type of disorder there are wide variations in how children respond in research experiments. Their responses in a research project could be varied with children providing both weak and strong responses to various research experiments. There has been both progress and setbacks in brain research from equipment failure, loss of research data as well as changes in professional staff who bring to a study different ideas about brain research and autism.

Questions to consider:
Is there a simplified way to explain complex brain research to parents who have autism concerns for their children?

What are some ways to make brain research results practical and helpful for the general public to gain a better understanding of autism?

Questionable Research Areas

The people who research and study autism has changed over the years. Where autism was once studied by educators, psychologists and doctors it is now studied by a variety of people in multiple fields of study. Some of this interest has come from the fact that autism has impacted so many families. As a result, many things have been linked to autism. A doctor studying medications may link autism to medications the mother took during pregnancy. A scientist studying vaccinations may try an link autism to vaccines. A social worker may link autism to a history of women who were abused. Communication professionals may be interested in connecting television watching or communication patterns to autism. Some researchers interested in environmental issues have studied topics like air pollution and have linked it to autism. Occupational therapist and vision specialists find interest in autism to motion and sensory issues. Sociologists and psychologists are linking autism to things like birth order or the age of the father or mother and are interested in finding out why autism affects boys more than girls. It is also interesting that computer specialists and engineers have shown an interest in autism research. Some have developed visual images to help children with autism respond to facial expressions of different emotions or just different visual patterns that children with autism may follow or respond to on a computer or electronic device. As you can see there are many questionable links to autism.

Questions to consider:
How does the researcher's professional background influence the direction and focus of autism research?

Do professionals with different training experiences and education focus on very limited aspects of autism or is the research focused on broader components of autism?

Questionable Change Related to Autism

Sometimes I will read and listen to discussions of people who indicate a child with autism has made a tremendous change and would no longer even be considered autistic because the change or improvement was so dramatic. Many things can account for changes in behavior, attitude, social interaction and communication from a number of societal factors. Sometimes I will hear a parent say that a change in diet did wonders in changing a child's responses and behaviors. I have talked to nurses who tell me a better diet and eating healthier foods will certainly help many children experiencing behavioral issues and not just autism concerns. The change is also seen in children who at first had unidentified allergies and then received treatment for addressing the allergies. Food allergies in particular can have a big impact on a children's behavior and their anxiety and irritability levels to complete tasks and participation in classroom routines. There are times a change may come from moving the child to a different classroom or how the child responds to a different teacher or therapist. Varying techniques or classroom management strategies may help the child respond in a different way or learn new social or communication skills. Other parents suggest that certain therapies and group sessions benefit and train the child to develop better social skills for interacting with others. Changes in behavior occur not only within children with autism, but in children with other disabilities.

Questions to consider:
Was a change in the child's behavior or actions directly related to a specific modification in diet, therapy, a strategy or a routine adjustment?

Is the change in the child's actions or behavior a long term or stable change or just a short term response to a new diet, therapy or modification?

Questionable Misunderstanding of Signs

There are times a parent or other adult may have a misunderstanding of a sign or symptom of autism. This takes a sensitive professional to explain and redirect the parent or adult to a different way of thinking. For instance, a parent might indicate the child is hand flapping, but a closer look by a nurse notices the child has hand tremors or what is sometimes described as an involuntary type of hand movement. Another example would be a child described as having autism because he or she lacks play interaction skills. The child who lacks play experiences or has had limited opportunities to interact with other children is different from the child with autism who may be unresponsive, standoffish or withdrawn from other children. Yet another possibility of a misunderstanding might be a child who has not developed a strong vocabulary, but uses meaningful gestures to show an interest in items as part of a language delay. Where as some children with autism characteristics don't use language directed toward others and the lack of language impacts social interaction skills. Some misunderstanding can be clarified easily by helping the parents observe the child's behavior in a different way. Other misunderstandings about autism may take a little more explanation for parents from professionals. Professionals can use a variety of means to educate parents such as brochures, question and answer sessions, informative talks, internet messages and personal discussions.

Questions to consider:
Are the child's deficit areas related specifically to autism or considered a different type of delay?

Does the parent have misunderstandings about autism signs that need to be explained more fully to clarify the child's possible autism signs and symptoms?

Chapter 6
Questionable Autism Field Issues

There are questionable field issues that need to be addressed in the autism area. Of course, in the autism field there are issues related to state regulations or guidelines and how procedural changes impact professionals and the families of children with autism. In addition to those issues the use of an advocate in autism eligibility meetings is explored as the chapter looks at the need for an autism advocate. Even when progress is noted by professionals there may be a need to be able to understand or question the progress the child is making in relation to the area of autism. The issue of the 'one symptom' autism claim is explored as professionals look at the abundance of characteristics related to autism versus only seeing one sign in a child and making a full determination about autism.

Another factor discussed in relation to professionals are stumbling blocks related to referrals, benefits, guidelines and paperwork that impact parents, children and families pursuing an autism diagnosis or educational eligibility of autism. These practical issues may include a look at inconsistent patterns of behavior in children, how information is miscommunicated by both professionals and parents and the child's awareness of surroundings across different settings. Other professional issues addressed include a look at obvious and not so obvious symptoms of autism, issues related to a child's progress and improvement as well as stumbling blocks in understanding autism. Field issues are impacted by guidelines that can change the view of autism in society.

Questionable Inconsistent Patterns

In looking at autism the professionals sometimes will note if the child has inconsistent patterns related to his or her responses, reactions and observations. A child may be over-responsive to some sensory experiences and on the other hand show no response or a lack of response to other situations. Professionals and teachers are usually trying to find out what things the child responds appropriately to and then work to help the child increase consistency with routines and daily activities. The more intensive interventions may be used to help redirect the child. This redirection or change can help the child with the inconsistent patterns. For instance, a teacher may think of ways to redirect the child and help him or her cope with sensitivity and the responsiveness of the child to certain classroom and home activities. In order to help children with autism concerns and inconsistent patterns of behavior an individualized approach is helpful. I once had a teacher of students with autism tell me her class was so diverse that she had to vary teaching techniques to many different levels. Children with autism definitely need different levels of support. The support can change if a student responds well and then needs limited support or is still having difficulty and needs a higher level of support. Some children will need more reinforcement or incentives to guide them back to more consistent responses, while other children can make substantial gains with a little redirection or a change in classroom routines.

Questions to consider:
What are some coping strategies to help children with autism concerns deal with inconsistent patterns of behavior?

What type of teacher support or classroom adaptations could help a child with autism become more consistent in the school environment?

Questionable Need for an Autism Advocate

It is optional to use an autism advocate at an eligibility meeting or to develop a child's individualized education program. Some parents choose to bring an advocate for support and advice while other parents handle these meetings on their own. It may depend on the parent's knowledge about the field of autism. Some parents want another person to confide in if they have questions that are not being answered, while other parents really have the ability to understand what is going on in this special education progress. One parent was a special education teacher and she brought an advocate to the meeting. However, after the meeting the parent commented that she really wished she had not used an advocate because she understood what was going on and the advocate made the meeting very long and intimidating. I have spoken with professionals who have been in many meetings with autism advocates. One experienced professional pointed out to me that the advocates often look for three things.

First, the eligibility of autism is examined and there is either agreement or disagreement on whether it is autism or another eligibility category. Second, the advocates seem to be very strong in commenting on the placement of the child in a particular type of program. Third, there seems to be questions about time such as the number of minutes and the actual time allotted for speech therapy. It is certainly a parent's personal choice to use an autism advocate or not.

Questions to consider:
Would an autism advocate benefit my understanding of the autism eligibility process and help in the educational planning for my child?

How do I go about finding an autism advocate (what agencies are in my community and what would the cost be) that could help me through the special education process ?

Questionable State Regulations

There are times when a child qualifies for special education or an eligibility of autism in one state and does not qualify for the same services in another state. States can determine what scores qualify for a disability in that state. It is very possible that a child may meet eligibility criteria in one state for autism and not in another state. This is very difficult for parents who may have just accepted an eligibility of autism in one state, to learn that professionals in another state view a disability or eligibility in another way. It causes parents to question which professionals in various states more closely determined the needs and eligibility for the child's concerns. Another area where state regulations impact parents is when the parent is asked to make a quick decision for services. The parent is given a lot of information at the eligibility meeting and if the child qualifies parents are asked if they want to develop an educational plan for the child. The parent in most cases has to decide at the meeting if they want to accept the services or not. I have seen some parents say 'I can't decide today,' 'Can I read this at home' or 'I just need more time to figure out all this information.' However, most regulations seem to emphasize agreeing to the idea to develop the plan right after the eligibility meeting to stay within the deadlines. Parents can of course change their mine and refuse services at a later time, but this does seem to put pressure on parents in relation to state regulations.

Questions to consider:
Is my child's eligibility of autism looked at the same if I move to a different state and how can I find out the state regulations?

What are some ways professionals can explain to parents why an autism eligibility or other special education eligibility has changed from state to state?

Questionable Miscommunication of Information

There are some terms floating around that that are confusing and can be part of miscommunication to parents when having conversations about autism. I have heard parents scuff at a doctor's comment the child has a 'slight case of autism.' One would wonder if the child has a few autistic like characteristics or if the child actually meets criteria for a diagnosis or a possibly an eligibility of autism. There are times when information from medical professionals is in miscommunication to the school district. Sometimes a parent will say my child has a diagnosis of autism from a doctor. However, on further review of medical records the child did not have a diagnosis of autism. The doctor may have mentioned to the parent something about autism and the parent misunderstood the information and mistook it as an actual autism diagnosis. There are times when a doctor will write in a report something like there is an impression of autism, but provide no detail or bases for that impression. Parents may also be confused of whether a child was tested for autism by a previous agency. Sometimes parents will say that a child has been tested and found to have autism, but on closer contact with the agency it is sometimes discovered that the child shows some developmental delays and autism was not tested or looked at from that agency. The school nurses and special education teachers in multi-team assessments have been great to help clarify some of the miscommunication of information.

Questions to consider:
Was information regarding a child's health, medical and early intervention history clearly communicated to the parent regarding the child's concern?

Are the professionals communicating information accurately regarding testing, diagnosis and possible concerns related to autism and other conditions?

Questionable Slow Procedure Changes

It seems like when there is a procedure or legal change it can take a couple of years before the actual changes take place in many school districts. There are times when the procedure changes are minimal so staff at schools may not feel the pain or it could be a change that only impacts a few school staff members. However, when there are major changes in educational eligibilities it can take more time to educate the staff members and make sure the school employees are on the same page as they start to implement the new changes. There can be changes in how paperwork is written and in how educational professionals explain the changes to parents. Many times state education agencies have to meet and redesign new codes and standards for the state. This takes time and numerous meetings to make policy changes. Once the changes are made by state agencies, the information has to be communicated to the local districts. The local school districts have to redesign forms to meet the new criteria or standards. Parent information must be rewritten, especially if there are legal documents or rights that are explained to the parents. Finally, staff at the local districts have to be trained to implement new procedures and recognize the changes from the current program. When staff members leave and new staff members are hired, it sometimes impacts the pace that changes are made in a system. Procedural changes do take time, but they should be done efficiently to get the correct information to staff and parents.

Questions to consider:

How do new changes in the law effect the autism eligibility programs in the schools and how does it impact children in the school district?

Will these procedure changes be implemented in a timely fashion and will these changes impact my child's placement in an autism classroom?

Questionable Awareness of Surroundings

A common autism thread to recognize autism awareness concerns or problems is whether the child's behavior or actions appear across settings. For example, children with autism who lack communication and social skills will probably show those deficits whether they are at home, in a daycare or at a preschool. If a child's awareness of the environment is more variable, it could be a sign the child may not have autism. A child with some socialization delays may change his or her behavior in different settings. For instance, a child may be naughty at home and fine in the preschool setting. On the other hand, a child may be warm and cooperative at home where he or she gets all of his or her needs met, but has major tantrums in a day care or preschool setting where demands and rules are placed on him or her. The shift of different behaviors and actions of the child in the environment shows that the child may have more awareness of the different settings and is more aware of different people in various surroundings. Professionals may notice this when assessing a child at different times. One professional may note the child is withdrawn, while another professional later in the day will say the child warmed up and was interactive and cooperative. The child's awareness of his or her behavior in various surroundings may indicate some type of social delay. Children with autism may tend to not have as much shifting behavior in the various settings.

Questions to consider:

Was the child's behavior consistent across settings or did the child present with variable behavior at different places and times?

Did the child make an attempt to communicate with others in different settings or was the child's behavior consistent or unchanging in different surroundings?

Questionable One Symptom Autism Claim

There have been times when autism concerns were based on a limited number of behaviors presented in the child. Autism eligibility criteria has changed over the years and taken on new directions. One particular change is that autism is not viewed as a particular behavior or trait, but it is seen more as a set or group of behaviors that reflect the characteristics of autism. There are times when parents notice a single symptom or sign related to a characteristic of autism and make major claims on that one symptom. For example, a parent may notice a single symptom such as a child who covers his or her ears or walks on his or her toes. If there is just one symptom the child may not have autism. Normally professionals are looking for an abundance of characteristics related to a child's communication, social interaction and restricted interests. If a child has only one characteristic of autism (and it would have to be severe), it would be very rare for a team of professionals to go with an eligibility of autism on one symptom or characteristic. In addition, a parent cannot rule out a characteristic like sensory issues which may or may not be related to autism. Sometimes the diagnosis or educational eligibility may require that the child shows deficits in more than one area with special emphasis related to the areas of social, communication and repetitive types of behaviors as well as restricted types of interests. Professionals are looking at these sets of behaviors to observe whether the child has persistent deficits and an abundance of characteristics related to autism.

Questions to consider:
Does my child just show one characteristic indicating autism or does he or she present with other traits of autism?

Did the professional get a broad picture of the child's deficits related to communication, social interaction, restricted interests and repeated types of behaviors?

Questionable Obvious Symptoms

There are some professionals who may identify a child with autism who has more significant or obvious symptoms of autism at a younger age. However, there are some children who show more subtle signs of autism that aren't obvious to most people or even some professionals. There are times when screeners, autism types of checklists and various autism scales just don't reveal the child's unique symptoms of autism. Sometimes a more specialized autism observation where professionals have had additional training is needed to really see if a child has symptoms of autism, delays or just typical behaviors. Not every symptom of autism is clear cut, especially in children with more mild types of symptoms. For example, some children may sound like they are using social greetings appropriately to one professional, but another professional may see the child using canned social greetings that are rote and memorized without a lot of meaning or comprehension of information. There are also inconsistencies in how some children exhibit both appropriate and inappropriate social interactions and communication patterns. Disagreements among professionals exist in how they view these inconsistencies in young children. Some professionals say go ahead and give an autism eligibility and then exit the child if he or she is making significant progress, while others would say let's go with a developmental delay eligibility and observe the child in the classroom setting to gain a fuller picture of the child's behavior, communication and social interaction with others.

Questions to consider:

Does the child have severe or mild symptoms that could cause someone to suspect autism or another condition?

Does the professional have the training or expertise to spot more subtle signs of autism when evaluating a child?

Questionable Autism Stumbling Blocks

When a medical or educational professional speculates concerns about autism to a parent there is a need to question what things influence this speculation or possibility of autism and address the stumbling blocks. There are also considerations and stumbling blocks of differing educational eligibility requirements in various states. Some of these speculations and decisions are related to the families' insurance companies and what services may or may not be paid for treatment related to autism. It is unfortunate when a doctor may suggest 'autism' as an easy answer without fully pursuing the autism concerns. There are very distinct and often varying opinions and points of view about autism from the medical and education professions. At other times, medical professional decisions are based on the opinions and decisions of a doctor to pursue a referral or testing related to autism or other conditions. For example, a nurse working in a diagnostic clinic makes a referral for a child to have a genetic evaluation. This referral may not be automatically recommended or completed because a doctor doesn't want to pursue the referral. Sometimes a referral is not completed because of the mountain of paperwork to be filled out by the doctors, medical or educational professionals. There may be insurance requirements, agency guidelines, state and federal standards and professional decisions that impact whether a referral is pursued or obtained to help a family receive answers about autism. When autism is speculated as a concern it must be looked at with the same persistence as other conditions.

Questions to consider:
Were all avenues for testing and evaluation pursued in determining my child's disorder or possible autism condition?

Are there stumbling blocks (e.g. insurance questions and referral issues) that need to be resolved to help the child receive a full evaluation for autism and other concerns?

Questionable Progress

Many times a parent will brag somewhat about the success the child is making and therefore want to reduce or even have the child be exited from special education services. There is a need to be cautious before making quick decisions to reduce or exit a child from special education services. For example, a child with autism may start using more words and show a stronger vocabulary following oral language interventions. A parent will quickly recognize this success as they remember when the child was not talking or communicating at all a year earlier. The parent may say to the teacher 'he is talking more' and I think he could be in a regular education program. However, the teacher may want to observe the child for a longer period of time to see if the child is comprehending the language, rather than just repeating or memorizing words. The parent may have to be encouraged to step back and give the teacher a little more time to look at the comprehension and pragmatic use of the child's language. Another issue is that a child may be responding in a very structured routine with lots of prompts and cues so it looks as if he is making fast progress. However, if that child is put into a classroom or school situation where teachers or staff use less prompting the child may have a reaction to the changing dynamics of a classroom. The child may have a setback and require reinforcement and a more structured placement rather than a regular education classroom. Parents must think through the options before making a request for a change in placement and look at the long term impact for the child.

Questions to consider:
Are issues about the child's progress and accomplishments discussed with team members (e.g. classroom teacher, speech therapist and school psychologist) and the parent?

Were placement options discussed with the parent to address other possibilities for a child with autism who is making progress and gains in an educational setting?

Questionable Avoidance of Autism

There are parents who do not want to accept the idea that their child has autism. Often these parents want to just avoid the whole idea of talking about autism. Some parents will say to the school psychologist things like 'could we just call it something else-not autism.' They might say 'just call it a sensory issue' and 'please don't use the word autism in the report to describe my child.' Sometimes parents will simply stop the diagnostic evaluation once autism concerns are brought up by educational professionals. The parent may refuse to complete the interview or checklist if he or she gets wind that the professionals are looking at the area of autism. At other times, the parent will pull a child from a public school and put him or her in a private preschool or school. The parent may not mention that the autism concern has previously surfaced from another evaluation. Some parents may want to avoid a diagnosis of autism because if may upset the career plans of a parent or the future career plans of the child. For instance, there are some branches of the military that would not allow a military transfer to a foreign country because the parents have a child with a handicap or autism eligibility. It could also limit the child's future opportunity to join military service as a career. There may be other careers that have limited opportunities if a person has a diagnosis of autism. Therefore, some parents may want to completely avoid a discussion about autism concerns in their child.

Questions to consider:
What future career opportunities are available or limited if my child has an educational eligibility or diagnosis of autism?

Did the professionals discuss with parents that autism is a spectrum type of disorder where not all children present with the exactly the same profile and concerns?

Questionable Left Out Information

There have been cases where information is omitted or not passed on to professionals from parents, agencies or other doctors. Sometimes there are missing pages or a speech report that leaves out autism concerns or tests and the partial report or recommendations only address speech concerns or vocabulary development. This can be misleading as a team may not address autism concerns because a complete report was not forwarded to the team members assessing the child. When home observation reports from early childhood developmental specialists are left out, clinicians cannot get pertinent information from specialists who worked directly with the child from a few months to several years. These observations can document how the child communicates with others or reacts to play and social experiences in the home. When children have had limited play experiences outside of the home, these in-home observation reports are important in developing a profile or picture of the child's strengths and weaknesses. Sometimes a parent withholds or fails to mention that a child was assessed in another state because the parent wants a more objective evaluation from a different group of professionals. In other cases, the parent is fully aware of a diagnosis of autism, but is in denial and does not want to address the educational concerns related to autism. However, missing or left out information can be a stumbling block for professionals who want to accurately assess a child for autism.

Questions to consider:
Were medical and agency reports requested from professionals who have assessed or worked directly with the child?

Was the medical or agency information received on the child complete or were there missing components in the report noted?

RECOMMENDED READING for AUTISM

Peterson, S. (2013). *Is my child autistic or delayed?* New York: Vilnius.

Is My Child Autistic or Delayed? is a book geared for parents and professionals to examine autism concerns and developmental delays in children. The book is parent friendly written in easy to understand language. It would also benefit college students learning to work with parents and early childhood students with delays and autism concerns. Parent concerns in many areas are presented from a school psychologist's perspective of the concern.

The book is also focused to help professionals as it gives an overview of different autism characteristics. *Is My Child Autistic or Delayed?* explores the multidisciplinary team approach in the decision making process of whether a child is delayed or has autism characteristics.

Is My Child Autistic or Delayed? is a wonderful resource for parents (and professionals) beginning the process of an educational assessment for possible autism concerns and developmental delays.

Is My Child Autistic or Delayed? is available in both print and ebook versions and was honored in the 2013 Global Ebook Awards program.

INDEX

A

Advocate, 63
Agency, 39
Assessment, 4,7
Attention, 28
Autism, 19, 55, 63, 70,72
Autism assessment, 1, 4
Autism characteristics, 27
Autism descriptors, 17
Autism disorders, 16
Autism increases, 53
Avoidance behaviors, 72
Awareness, 67

B

Behavior, 22,27,47
Behavioral issues, 27
Brain research, 56

C

Causes, 54
Change, 29,58, 66
Changes, 66

Checklist, 39
Confusing, 46
Confusion, 40, 46
Consideration, 22
Consultation, 19
Criteria, 15
Cueing, 33

D

Decision, 33
Delays, 18, 20, 32, 46
Determination, 8
Developmental delays, 20, 32
Developmental specialist, 28
Diagnosis, 16, 18
Differences, 14
Disability, 21
Disorder, 21, 50

E

Early childhood, 43
Eligibility, 3, 14, 18, 21, 42, 52
Experience, 7
F
Family, 26
Field, 61
Funding allocations, 9
79

G

Genetic condition, 50
Genetic evaluation, 50

H

History, 26
Home interventions, 19

I

Immaturity, 30
Improvement, 55
Inconsistent, 23, 62
Information, 23, 65, 73
Interests, 28
Interventions, 17, 43
Issues, 25, 61

J

Justification, 27
K
Knowledge, 15, 28, 80

L

Lack of knowledge, 15
Lacking Skills, 41
Length, 4
Lifelong, 21

M

Medical diagnosis, 13
Method, 2
Milestone, 32
Miscommunication, 65
Misunderstanding, 59

Multiple categories, 52

N

Neurodevelopment, 51

O

Observable behaviors, 47
Obsevation, 22
Obvious symptoms, 69
One symptom, 68
Outdated, 5
Overcueing, 33, 81

P

Patterns, 62
Philosophy, 44
Phrases, 34
Placement, 45
Planning, 42
Practices, 37
Pressured decision, 35
Program philosophy, 38
Professional issues, 13
Progress, 71
Protocols, 5, 6

Q

Questionable, 1-68

R

Reactions, 31
Regression, 42
Reporting information, 11
Reporting, 10
Research links, 49, 57
Rise of autism, 20

S

Safety, 18
Screener, 8
Screening 1
Screening approaches, 9, 82
Scores, 10
Sensory awareness, 27, 31
Sensory issues, 31
Setting, 29
Signs, 59
State regulations, 64
Support, 29, 42
Surroundings, 67
Syndrome, 19

T

Team approach, 3
Testing, 1, 2
Training, 7

U

Umbrella term, 17
Unclear criteria, 16
Updated, 6

Susan Louise Peterson

Afterword

If autism concerns could be easily addressed there would be no need for this book. What really stands out for me is that sometimes autism is not questioned until years later. Parents may readily accept an autism eligibility from a school district or a medical diagnosis of autism without question. However, a few years later when a child has made incredible educational progress and the school decides to totally exit the child out of a special education program, the parent may start to question if autism was really the key issue for the child or if there was another type of delay or disorder that better described the child. The field of autism is sometimes seen as 'cloudy' or filled with 'muddy water' so there is definitely a need to question and keep questioning how autism can be clarified for both parents and professionals.

www.ingramcontent.com/pod-product-compliance
Lightning Source LLC
Chambersburg PA
CBHW060502080526
44584CB00015B/1516